On this special day _____

_____

Received First Holy Communion

At

_____

Church   Priest Presiding

_____

God Parents

_____

My prayer for you: _____

_____

_____

By:

_____

My prayer for you: _____

_____

_____

By:

_____

My prayer for you: _____

_____

_____

By:

_____

My prayer for you: _____

_____

_____

By:

_____

My prayer for you: _____

_____

_____

By:

_____

My prayer for you: _____

_____

_____

By:

_____

My prayer for you: _____

_____

_____

By:

_____

My prayer for you: _____

_____

_____

By:

_____

My prayer for you: _____

_____

_____

By:

_____

My prayer for you: _____

_____

_____

By:

_____

My prayer for you: _____

_____

_____

By:

_____

My prayer for you: _____

_____

_____

By:

_____

My prayer for you: _____

_____

_____

By:

_____

My prayer for you: _____

_____

_____

By:

_____

My prayer for you: _____

_____

By:

_____

My prayer for you: _____

_____

By:

_____

Reception: _____

_____

_____

Hosted By:

_____

Special Food: _____

_____

_____

By:

_____

Special Gift: _____

_____

_____

Given By:

_____

Special Gift: _____

_____

_____

Given By:

_____

Special Gift: _____

_____

_____

Given By:

_____

Special Gift: _____

_____

_____

Given By:

_____

Special Gift: _____

_____

_____

Given By:

_____

Special Gift: _____

_____

_____

Given By:

_____

Special Gift: _____

_____

_____

Given By:

_____

Special Gift: _____

_____

_____

Given By:

_____

Special Gift: _____

_____

_____

Given By:

_____

Special Gift: _____

_____

_____

Given By:

_____

Special Gift: _____

_____

_____

Given By:

_____

Special Gift: _____

_____

_____

Given By:

_____

Special Gift: _____

_____

_____

Given By:

_____

Special Gift: _____

_____

_____

Given By:

_____

Special Gift: _____

_____

_____

Given By:

_____

Special Gift: _____

_____

_____

Given By:

_____

Special Gift: _____

_____

_____

Given By:

_____

Special Gift: _____

_____

_____

Given By:

_____

My First Communion Special Celebration!

Guest Book, Photographs, Well Wishes, Memories

Copyright © 2017 The Catholic Sacramental Supply Company

No part of this publication may be reproduced in any format, photocopied, digitally transmitted or otherwise copied in any way. All art within is copyrighted. Gstudio-Fotolia, Daisy.bee-Fotolia, Tom15- Fotolia, Tomas Rzymkiewicz-Fotolia.

Made in the USA
Middletown, DE
22 April 2017